UK's NO. 1 HAPPINESS COACH
DR KENNY AKINDELE-AKANDE

FINDING HAPPINESS

Learn How to Stay on Top of Your Game in 30 Days

authorHOUSE®

AuthorHouse™ UK
1663 Liberty Drive
Bloomington, IN 47403 USA
www.authorhouse.co.uk
Phone: 0800.197.4150

Published by AuthorHouse 06/24/2017

ISBN: 978-1-5246-8264-4 (sc)
ISBN: 978-1-5246-8265-1 (e)

Contents

FOREWORD

As researcher in Cardiovascular Medicine, finding happiness is very essential for healthy living. The world today is full with crisis that sometimes gets us confused and overburdened, causing unhappiness, which Dr. Akande's message articulates the need to find happiness amidst life's misfortunes and uncertainty. The effects of fall on the heart. The heart appears to be the organ that suffers most from increasing life's miseries, and this sometimes could cause heart attack, heart failure and even diabetic, which many people suffer from today.

This dynamic young and hardworking Happy Life Coach has provided outstanding strategies and extraordinary vision to empower her readers.

DR. MARK AMADI RESEARCHER IN CARDIOVASCULAR MEDICINE

Give yourself the gift and spend the next 31 days to finding true happiness to live a rich and purposeful life!

Dr Kenny provides you the important life affirming reminders, reflections and daily meditations to guide you on this journey of discovery.

So make it the first thing you do each morning when you wake up!

Because Dr Kenny lives and breathes this and is an awesome example and role model of what you can achieve when you do!

DR ROSS MCKENZIE – FOUNDER & CEO, THE STARTUP BUSINESS & THE STARTUP BUSINESS SCHOOL

I encourage you to read this book as it teaches you to reflect on your life positively with a determination to move forward. It empowers you with the ability to own your life, stay on top of your game and build beneficial relationship to achieve your desired greatness. Dr Kenny's mind-blowing message on Happiness also shows how right ATTITUDE plays a significant role in finding HAPPINESS.

SIMON COULSON – FOUNDER OF THE INTERNET BUSINESS SCHOOL. AUTHOR OF AMAZON NO.1 BESTSELLER 'INTREPRENEUR'.

Dr Kenny is a writer whose material will inspire you to higher heights, no matter who you are in the society.

Her passion and joy is to see people succeed.

This is a profound insightful book.

You can feel her passion through this book which I believe will trigger your search for true happiness.

This book is truly inspirational and life changing in application.

I will highly recommend this book to anyone in search of true happiness.

Thank you Dr Kenny for superb work with practical applications, which I believe will eventually lead to a life transforming experience.

PASTOR YEMI BALOGUN. PRESENTER/PRODUCER AT REVELATION TV, FINEST CHRISTIAN TV STATION IN EUROPE.

WHY DID I WRITE THIS BOOK FOR YOU

You might have been surviving all these time, it is high time you started living. Not just living but enjoys living. It is about time that the new version of you emerges.

Happiness comes from knowing your life is not stagnant, that at each phase of life, you are evolving into something new and fresh, which brings joy and zest to your life.

True happiness comes from the realization of the joy within, rooted in discovering and knowing who we are. What we possess or long to be don't define us, our true identity lies deep within us.

Many people struggle with unhappiness, identity crises, hurts and pains and yet they still have to continue to live, expected to be perfect in their relationships, fulfill obligations at work and so on.

No one cares to be patient enough to see through the outer covering and reach out to help them. Can't really blame anyone, everyone has got their cross to carry. That is one of the reason I wrote this book, to do-it-yourself-, help yourself find the happiness you deserve.

Are you longing, search for identity and a yearning to discover who you really want to be?

That is another reason I wrote this book. Trust me, I have been there, I am not just giving theory, I am introducing you to the practicality of my journey to happiness.

Are you ready to love yourself enough to take actions required for your happiness?

READING THIS BOOK IS ONE OF THE BEST DECISION YOU MADE THIS YEAR.

MEET THE Author

Dr. Kenny Akindele-Akande
{The UK's No.1 Happy Life Coach}

Born and bred in Lagos, Nigeria, Dr. Kenny is a Dentist, A Life Performance Coach and Motivational Speaker. Certified and registered Master Coach with Coaching Standard Authority UK and a directory member of Associate Professional for Trainers, Coaches and Consultants {APTCC} UK.

"Dr. Kenny" has called by friends, family and colleagues is a compassionate listener and coach. For five years, she has listened to her client's problem and had devised strategies to combat their problem.

She will be sharing many of these strategies in this book.

Asides Coaching, Dr. Kenny is an excellent Public Speaker {in various events} and Presenter. She has motivated friends and family and people 1-2-1 and through her live broadcast on social media.

Dr. Kenny had run number of seminars and workshops for teenagers and young people. She had also had a diploma in Child Psychology and Youth Coaching, which gave her a rounded knowledge to deal with young people. The events are:

"Gems and Jewel Teenage Club"

"Beautiful Brainy and Godly club for girls"

"Purpose Driven Moms"

She had just incorporate Falling in Love with Destiny's Motivational training for individual and corporate clients along with running its flagship events and workshops,

"1 DAY WORKSHOP FINDING HAPPINESS…how to stay on top of your game"

"SHE…let every woman rise! Workshops for women".

Dr. Kenny's drive and passion lies in helping people realize their true potentials and discover their purpose and destiny. Which is why she was inspired to write this book, to give answer to the troubling question most people are asking. "Why I'm I here on earth?" or "How can I find happiness?".

In this book, Dr. Kenny broadly discussed her own built system and life applicable strategies that will help anyone derive happiness and stay happy for the rest of their lives on earth.

She also brilliantly used quotes to brighten the knowledge of these strategies and to buttress her point.

Dr. Kenny, through her background in Science and Psychology included outstanding researches, scientific phenomena and laws to drive home her point.

You are in for a great time…

AUTHOR'S SPEECH

NEW YOU...NEW VERSION

Many times, opportunities come around us but we don't see them because they are disguised and wrapped with challenges.

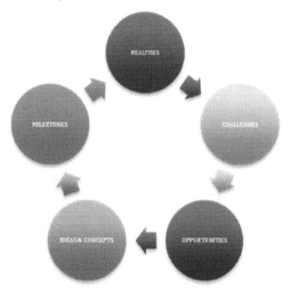

- Opportunities
- Milestones
- Challenges
- Ideas & Concept
- New version came wrapped up with all these factors.

Opportunities come around us everyday, challenges are inevitable in life and nature gracefully grants us ideas and concept waiting to become reality only if we work at them.

Opportunities come around us everyday, but we miss them because of our foolish pursuit of happiness and fulfillment; meanwhile what you are looking for is around us.

I'm a Life Coach; I coach people to be the BEST version of themselves.

- This book is about helping you discover the latest and updated version of You.

- This book is a 30-DAY JOURNEY TO FINDING TRUE HAPPINESS.

- Are you searching for happiness in the wrong places, platforms and with wrong people?

- It is about DISCOVERY of YOU.

- This book will help you create your own happiness.

- It is divided into four with three basic systems that had worked for me and I will be introducing them to you.

- The first one is Gratitude System

- The second is Live Large Strategy

- The third is Purpose & Passion System

- The fourth will be Happiness projects, reflections and activities.

It is not death most people are afraid of but is getting to the end of life, only to realize that you never truly lived.

The reason why many lived and die unhappy will be expounded in this book. I have gracefully provided you a highway to unhappiness.

Come with me as I take you on a transformational journey of happiness.

HAPPINESS PROJECTS

In contemporary life, we often lose ourselves in the hustle and bustle … somewhere between the commute home and falling onto bed tired … we lose sight of our dreams and who we want to become.

When slowing down is not an option, it makes sense to carve a little time out of our day … the wasted time in between lunch making needless calls … the time spent waiting for dinner to be ready or to finally fall asleep on the bed. This is where happiness project comes in: you can slot in; you can slot in in at these moment or at the end of each day for reflection, exercise or affirmation.

This happiness book combines great insights, quotes, best mindfulness, positive psychology and neuroscience. Happiness project have been placed at the end of each chapter, they are experimental activities, worksheets and guide to implement what has been learnt from each day.

It will also provide step-by-step solutions to day-to-day living, reduce stress and empower individual in pursuit of happiness.

Happiness Realities

- Happiness is a choice

- As we engage in the custom that promotes happiness, we can begin to change our rigid perspective and train our brains to be happier.

- More happiness stimulates good health, efficiency, big-heartedness, empathy and resilience

- Lifestyles of happiness will eventual send a ripple effect into your circle of friends and family.

- Happiness project will be at the end of each day or chapter, a time I will advice you set aside to reflect, practice and affirm yourself.

This time will be used to discover who we are and get to know what the deepest desires of our heart truly are.

We only have one life … and to waste it not knowing what we want is a crime against ourselves.

Anonymous

Gratitude is the *1 way to improve your life.

Gal Lyne Goodwin

Gratitude changes the way we look at the world.

Anonymous

GRATITUDE SYSTEM

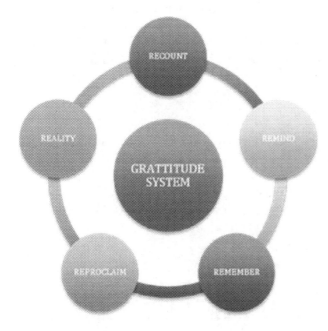

Life is a gift....

As human, we have a very difficult time acknowledging how much we've accomplished, how far we have come and battles we have won but we always recount our failures, negativity and shortcomings. Our positive qualities are just as real as our negative ones. We don't believe in our positive attributes because we have so much history and meaning invested in our negative aspects of self. That's because they're usually the stories we hear ourselves repeating.

Many are ungrateful to life for reasons of their present situation, failures and disappointments. And circumstance.

This Gratitude system will help you discover the fullness of life, will shift your perspective, move you into a higher frequency and attract good things to you.

Enjoy Life.

It is a gift.

Unwrap it with gratitude and happiness Kenny Akindele-Akande

GRATITUDE VERSUS THE PRIZE

So many times, our eyes are so on the prize of only what we want but also what we haven't yet achieved in order to arrive at what we want. This way of thinking makes us forget what we have.

What if you gave someone a gift, and they neglected to thank you for it-would you be likely to give them another? Life is the same way. In order to attract more blessings that life has to offer, you must truly appreciate what you already have.

Ralph Marston

Instead of being grateful for what we already have, we beat ourselves over and over again over target we could not meet. We judge ourselves on what we have not yet accomplished or "failed" at experiencing.

We forget to acknowledge what we've done to get us here today. Right here. Right now. We don't celebrate where we've had openings or victories or pushed through fears or how we've really transformed our lives.

WHY DO YOU NEED TO BE GRATEFUL?

Be grateful for your life…Every detail of it…and your face will come to shine like a sun…and everyone who sees it…will be made glad and peaceful. Rami

LIFE IS A JOURNEY

We are so often caught in the destination we desire that we fail to appreciate the journey. Get inspired by the experience of life and appreciate every person either amazing or not, they have come to play a role in your life. Enjoy the wonderful feeling, don't ignore it.

WITH GRATITUDE SYSTEM, I WANT TO SHOW FOUR THINGS

1. I want to show you how to set your life on a **5-DAY JOURNEY OF TRANSFORMATION**.

2. I want to help you create an attitude of gratitude.

3. How to allow your life resonate with gratitude to attract good things into your world.

4. Gratitude can bring Happiness that you long for.

In the next five days, I will advise you look for 30 minutes in the morning and 30 minutes at night to practice the Happiness project that comes at the end of each day.

Concentrate on counting your BLESSINGS

And you'll have little time to count anything else.

Count your blessings instead of your crosses;

Count your gains instead of your pains;

Count your grosses instead of your losses.

Count your joys instead of your woes;

Count your friends instead of your foes.

Count your smiles instead of your tears;

Count your courage instead of your fears;

Count your full years instead of your leans;

Count your kind deeds instead of your mean.

Count your health instead of your wealth

Count your better instead of your bitter

Count your love instead of your hate

Love your neighbor as much as yourself.

DAY 1
RECOUNT

Have you ever taken time out to recount how good life has been to you? But you, like many of us, are engrossed and blinded by the present situation that you can't just see beyond.

Can you remember how you narrowly escape death, how it was only you that didn't die in that car crash.

Or you miraculous got that dream job or house

How you were favored in places you didn't deserve to stand.

The list is endless.

So many times our eyes are set on the prize of the moment that we forget the medals of the past. How we won, how awesome you did and how far you have come in life.

Concentrate on counting your blessings and you will have little or no time to count anything else.

GRATITUDE IS LIKE A MUSCLE

The more you use it, the stronger it grows and the bigger it becomes. When you are grateful, you have tendency to draw more blessings and favours of life to yourself.

GRATITUDE IS LIKE FAITH

Through its effect cannot be seen with physical eyes, but it's result don't go unnoticed. It is evident. As you grow in gratitude, the more power you acquire to practice it more.

DAY 1 HAPPINESS PROJECT

Take 30 minutes today to reflect on your blessings, successes and past victory.

DAY 2
REMIND

You are welcome to Day 2.

Today is about bringing good memories to life in your mind. You will be reminding yourself of the emotions how you felt those days when Life was good to you.

I was coaching a lady who just came to a conclusion that life has not be fair to her. She was been deeply hurt by her ex-lover, the experience left her broken and shattered.

She would not smile to anyone or accept gesture.

I told her to give me permission to walk the next 5 days of her life with her, that if nothing changes she could give up.

BLESSING LIST

Now, we came up with a list of past and present blessings and goodness of life,

I asked to cast her mind back to when she was young, to remember experiences of growing up in a family, the love and attention you received in all her relationships.

Her best days in school, great moments with friends, in particular, I asked her, if there had been any man who loved and appreciated her before.

We discussed each of those moment, we focused on each of them, brought up all the happy juices one after the other, {through the knowledge of hypnotherapy}.

Thankfully, Her mood began to change, she began to smile and later burst out with a big laughter.

She even began to remember more and more things that were not on the list, she broke down in tears and concludes she has been ungrateful.

THE OUTCOME

Many a times, we allow present pressing situation decide who we are. We look in the mirror, we can't find that happy and joyous fellow we use to be. People look at us and they wander what went wrong. Life is full of ups and downs, when life is up, we are happy and joggling but when the ride dives down, it takes toil on us. Therefore we are allowing the tides of life determine our flow.

LAW OF MEDITATION

MEDITATION

Meditation is a practice where an individual trains the mind or induces a mode of consciousness, either to realize some benefit or for the mind to simply acknowledge its content without becoming identified with that content. **En.m.wikipedia.org**

Meditation may also involve creating an emotional state for the purpose of analyzing that state—such as anger, hatred, etc.—or cultivating a particular mental response to various phenomena, such as compassion.

RESEARCH ON MEDITATION

Research has shown that meditation has many mental and physical health benefits.

1. It may help reduce stress

2. Enhance concentration

3. Improve sleep

4. Manage pain

5. Lower blood pressure

BENEFITS OF MEDITATION

Meditation has a reassuring and comforting effect when practiced. It focuses consciousness inward to achieve inward purity and awakening. It tends to knob you of the past hurtful feelings and it directs your attention to just the PRESENCE.

Mindful meditation will help you to focus on the present, only on the present.

Anonymous

MINDFULNESS MEDITATION

"Mindfulness is the awareness that arises by paying attention on purpose in the present moment and non-judgmentally"

Jon Kabat-Zinn founder the Center for Mindfulness

"Mindfulness is the awareness that arises out of intentionally paying attention in an open, kind and discerning way"

Shuana Shapiro, leading researcher in the science of mindfulness.

As against the mindfulness meditation (adaptation from traditional Buddhist practices), which focuses on the present and not the past, Remind {one of the 5R's of Gratitude} is to help extract and use the elements and goodness of the past to encourage and give hope for the present and future.

Casting the mind back in meditation is not bad in itself, but it depends on the picture you want to capture. The picture that will help to achieve happiness in the present.

The discovery from this exercise will help you fuel the motion for the future. And to strengthen every of your weakness. It will also help you to always see the good and the bright side of life.

The practice of mindfulness will improve our lives when it is incorporated into daily activities: while eating, walking, talking and in relationship.

BRING LIGHT AND AWARENESS TO YOUR MOMENTS

For "daily life" meditation, the practice is to pay attention to what is going on in the present moment, to be aware of what is happening – and not living in "automatic mode". If you are speaking, that means paying attention to the words you speak, how you speak them, and to listen with presence and attention. If you are walking, that means being more aware of your body movements, your feet touching the ground, the sounds you are hearing, Anonymous

LAWS OF ATTRACTION

What you think, you create

What you feel, you attract

What you imagine, you become.

Anonymous

Law of Attraction responds to energy. Intentions and words have energy; once you know what you want and you state it, the universe conspires on your behalf through the Law of attraction.

Law of Attraction Experiment by GINA SENDEF

Gina Sendef demonstrated an experiment on meditation. It explained that within a timeframe when you have an immediate need, the Law of attraction works just as well as it does with longer-term goals; you are always manifesting!

"Ask the universe for a gift within the next 24 hours. That's it."

"Pay attention, because your gift might be subtle. " Said Gina.

Gina carried out experiment for the first time when she was on a very crowded and very delayed flight. Right after she stated the intention, she ordered a glass of wine from the flight attendant and when she went to hand her card to pay, the attendant said "don't worry, it's a gift".

Gina was amazed! "My gift came within almost an instance. Now, whenever I am in a funk, I ask the universe for a gift to lift my spirits and I've received lots of fun surprises!" Gina exclaimed. It is awesome that just by desiring something, a positive energy can be sent out to attract that thing to someone. It's amazing!

DAY 2 REMIND MEDITATION PROJECT

TOOLS

Memories

Pictures

Texts messages

Old emails

Certificates of achievement

Awards

SET A TIME

Your routine first thing in the morning sets the pace for the entire day. Early in the morning generally a good time to meditate. Before taking your bath, eating breakfast or before you get busy. Very early in the morning or late at night. You can start with 15 minutes and gently move up to 30 minutes or even an hour.

REASON: The reason for this is that we want to use the quiet moments of this two

Time slot to drive you into deep meditation.

SPACE AND POSTURE

Take a comfortable posture

      a. Lying down on the bed or

      b. Sitting in a yogic posture

REASON: to help relax your body and soul.

TAKE A GOOD BREATH AND MAINTAIN IT

STEP 1

Breathing relaxes the mind and body so you can calmly respond to the world around you.

Just follow a few breaths, in and out, about one minute without judgment.

STEP 2

Shut your eyes to prevent your mind from being distracted by surrounding objects.

STEP 3

Allow your breath to slowly deepen as you inhale and fully inflate your lungs, counting silently to four. Feel your ribcage expand forward and to the sides as you breathe in.

DIVE INTO THE GOOD MEMORIES

Go through the good memories one after the other.

Enjoy the moment it brings

Flavour the juice of the moment with some burst of laughter

Stay on meditating until you get your joy back.

MY EXPERIENCE WITH A CLIENT

Last year, I coached a guy, who was feeling dull and worthless after he was fired from a dream job.

I explained this REMIND MEDITATION CHALLENGE in one of his appointment with me.

I asked him to look at every certificate and pictures he ever had from childhood till date

Pictures of graduation

Successes

Failures

And most importantly, the success of the moment.

Look at all of these memories before starting the meditation. He did everything to the latter.

OUTCOME

You will be amazed by what what we discovered in this process. This guy, who was dejected, broken and feeling worthless, came back with a broad smile and new energy. He is happy to face life once again.

MEETING FACE-2-FACE WITH GOOD MEMORIES

Some might want to take it further by visiting the place of good memories.

Old family house, former primary or high school, wedding hall, former university.

Hanging out with old friend or family is a good one too, make sure they are positive relationship that will help you achieve your outcome, which is strength and happiness.

DAY 3
REMEMBER

Have you ever set a goal or have a mental picture of a good thing? and lo and behold it came to you. You didn't even have to ask anyone or work or stress yourself for it. The experience of joy I had in those seasons when life brought what I don't deserve, helped me through those times I'm pressured by desire to get something I felt I deserved and it is not coming forth. I had a simple experience a while ago.

I can remember in the year 2013, I was just thinking of getting this beautiful dress, in fact went online and put it in the cart and hopefully wish to buy it later.

And it was a friend, who knocked on my door and brought the exact size; I didn't discuss that with her or with anyone.

I felt humbled that day. That is amongst many other things that I didn't pray for.

Another one, I can remember setting a goal to be a doctor has a child, being ambitious. The dream looks so far fetched. In fact, not just me, my twin brother and I want to be a doctor and our father was scared of how would he cope with the finance plus we had four other siblings.

I remember he took us to one of his friends, to help convince us to change our minds, but we were adamant.

A year later, our father died and we were devastated, when we had a father, the dream of becoming doctors was blur now that he is gone, what will happen.

But the unexpected happened, that turn the story into a memory that I can't forget.

Good and wonderful people rally round my family, took care of us, paid our school fees, catered for us and that dream came alive.

I can remember the joy that flooded my heart when I took the Hippocratic oat before 5,000 guests at my induction at the medical school.

We won…

I became a doctor against all odds, losing not just my father at 16, but my mom at 23, this time I was preparing for first anatomy test in year 3, also a significant year in medical school.

Yes, we did conquer.

Anytime I am down, I always intentionally bring back those beautiful emotions I felt in those times, then I'd feel so full, grateful and satisfied. The experience was special to me and because of that I felt no further in life.

DAY 3 HAPPINESS PROJECT

1. Today, Remember goals that you set in the past that had come through. Successes and achievements of the past.

2. Think of the sweet experience and the moment you had in those times…

3. Now place those sweet moments side by side with the new goals and projects that may be challenging now.

Those worries are going to frizzle out and melt away in the presence of those joyful memories.

DAY 4
REPROCLAIM

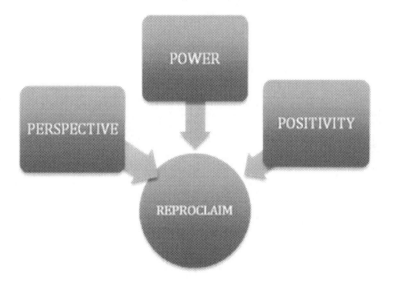

REPROCLAIM

This is a more active R. In Reproclaim,I will be discussing how you can talk about and display life's goodness to you.

This is a formula that works like magic.

Proclaim means announce publicly and officially. This looks more like the power of focus I talked about under meditation, only that proclaim involves positive, powerful confessions about you, your situation and future.

Gratitude system teaches you to derive positive thoughts and feelings from the first "R" remind and then go ahead and profess those good thoughts.

Everything is energy.

Your thought begins it,

Your emotions amplifies it

And your action increases the momentum.

Anonymous

I began to pay close attention to gratitude sometimes in 2016; I began to see life through a new perspective. I made up my mind to talk about the goodness of God and how life has been good to me regardless of the present challenges.

I will intentionally walk up to people and start a to gist on how good God has been, and the blessings life has offered me even when I didn't appreciate.

After awhile, I began to feel I have been so ungrateful and unworthy for many years.

Reproclaim gave me a new perspective, new energy and new action point.

REPROCLAIM GAVE ME NEW:

1. **Perspective**
2. **Power**
3. **Positivity**

PERSPECTIVE

I began to see new perspective to life; I began to focus on my inner drive and passion rather than profession. I went on a journey of discovering of who I truly am and who I am meant to be rather than what I want to be.

I knew truly within me while growing up that I was going to be a profound author, a public speaker, I love to teach and coach people.

I didn't have enough time to fan that passion into flame because the standard of academics in the world I belong to. There is so much focus on academics and just little on the talents and passion a child might have.

Academically I wanted to be a doctor but passion-wise, I have that gift of teaching-imparting knowledge. I do use that gift but I never saw a big picture through it. I see it as a side thing.

But now, the experience is different; I love it all the way.

Writing this book is a giant stride from that discovery.

POWER:

{Energy. Vigour. Momentum}

Quantum physics define Energy as the ability to do work.

Work is force times distance.

Energy to face life once again, to work on your goals daily comes from this PROCLAIM exercise.

Energy, new vigour and momentum to lead a grateful and purposeful life.

GAIN MOMENTUM, KEEP MOVING

In physics, momentum is the property or tendency of a moving objects to continue moving. For an object moving in a line, the **momentum** is the mass of the object multiplied by its velocity.

Momentum is the quantity of motion of a moving body. In a basic sense, the more momentum a moving object has, the harder it is to stop. The term is mostly used metaphorically like in the example of the sports team. It means the team is on a roll (generally, a winning streak) and is becoming a stronger team for it. The other teams will have a harder time stopping the team gaining momentum.

More than power or energy, you need to gain momentum to be on and stay on the move.

Don't second-guess your victory now, you have come a long way, we are making progress with GRATITUDE.

POSITIVE CONFESSION

I shall always stay positive

I shall no longer allow negative thoughts or feelings

To drain me of my energy.

Instead I shall focus on all the good that is in my life.

I will think it, feel it and speak it.

By doing so I will send out

Vibes of positive energy into

The world and I shall be grateful

For all the wonderful things it

Will attract into my life

www.mindfulwishes.com

POSITIVITY

It is time to get positive about life. Don't allow negative thoughts. Remember "your thoughts

Become feelings, feelings become actions and actions manifest as reality.

Kenny Akindele-Akande

A positive attitude brings much gratitude!

Think POSITIVE,

Speak POSITIVE

And stay POSITIVE!

Do it everyday

And do it Big

KUSHANDWIZDOM

When you think in terms of negativity you contract. Contraction collapses in on itself. It shrinks. It hides. It retracts our energy. Often in life we doubt, we second-guess, we apologize, and we get scared to take the leap.

Anonymous

Stay positive; turn your negative talks to positive profession.

Kenny Akindele-Akande

POSITIVE RIPPLE EFFECT

Positivity leads to expansion, expansion radiates outward. It magnifies. It energizes. It multiplies. It reinvigorates. It has a ripple affect and the pure physics of expansion means that we more positively influence greater numbers of people.

When you are happy, you dissipate positive force that attracts people to you. People want to hang around positive-minded person, the person who will laugh, celebrate and share with them. No one would tarry long with someone who is full of negativity, always complaining and can't see pass their pain.

Negativity drains energy, it also burst happy bubbles. So don't give it a chance in your mind.

Kenny Akindele-Akande

DAY 4 REPROCLAIM PROJECT

Profess this 20 I AM positive confession today.

You will observe a positive energy rising in you and sure confidence to face your world again.

I AM CONFESSION

I am grateful for life

I am thankful for all my blessings

I am appreciative of all my relationships

I am blessed

I am victorious

I am a conqueror

I am a winner

I am strong

I am powerful

I am creative

I am beautiful

I am wise

I am innovative

I am Kind

I am secured

I am resourceful

I am loving

I am compassionate

I am courteous

I am respectful

I AM FREE TO BE WHO I WANT TO BE

Kenny Akindele-Akande

DAY 5
REALITY

Today, I want to show you why you need to focus on the Reality of who you really are.

Taking the journey from the 4R's till now, Life is feeling much lighter, the burdens are getting lifted, I guess by now you are becoming radiant and you begin to appreciate what good is in the present moment and appreciate your challenges because they will soon become testimonies.

Then the reality of who you really are and what you should be begin to roll in.

LAWS OF FOCUS

Law Of Focus

It states "what you think expand. When you focus on positive things, you push your mind in the positive direction, your inner voice turns positive, and your life starts to improve". David J. Abott

It is important you focus on this new reality you have now. You are not where you use to be. You have made a steady commendable progress from Recounting your blessings, to Reminding and Remembering the good memories.

You have reproclaimed your goals and promises and visions for life. Now, the reality of your expectations is here. You have achieved greatness. Which is the discovering of a grateful person you have become. Focus on your REALITY.

You are a grateful fellow
You are confident
You are strong
You are making progress

You are a grateful fellow
You are significant
You are powerful
You are ready to take your world.

Kenny Akindele-Akande

SEVENTH LAW OF KARMA

The seventh Law of Karma is Law of focus.

It states "you can't be in two places at once. This means that you cannot be focused on pain and bitterness and expect to be happy.

Therefore, you have to make a choice between the two.

This explains that you only experience what you focus on. Can you frown and smile at the same time?

DAY 5 HAPPINESS PROJECT

EXPERIMENT

To prove that when energy is focused at a point, a cutting edge outcome is achieved.

The sharp point of a screwdriver allows you to direct energy of your arm movements on a much smaller surface so that you are able to accomplish much more than you could by expanding the same energy using a blunt surface.

RESULT

Screwdriver can cut more easily when it is sharper. Therefore, energy becomes more and more powerful the more you focus on it.

GO ON AND TRY THIS EXPERIMENT

TOOLS

A sharp screwdriver
A spoon
A cardboard {a cereal box}
A sheet of paper and pen

RULE 1

Pick up the cardboard box and try to stab it with your spoon.
Record your findings
Note how much energy dissipated before piercing it.

RULE 2

Now pick up the card box again and try pierce it with the screwdriver.
Record your findings.
Note how much energy expended this time around.

OUTCOME

The surface of the spoon is diffused. When it was used it to stab a box, the energy spreads out to many directions.
However, the screwdriver is focused. A lesser amount of energy will produce a much greater result.
What you just experienced now **is** a concentrated energy

HAPPINESS APPLICATION

What is the lesson drawn from this experiment?
We can apply this same principle to our lives in the journey to finding happiness.

DAY 6
REVISION 5 R'S TO GRATITUDE SYSTEM

In case you are wandering "where we are?", will quickly recap our 5-day journey.

*1 RECOUNT

Concentrate on counting your blessings and you will have little or no time to count anything else.

*2 REMIND

Remind yourself of the emotions how you felt those days when Life was good to you.

*3 REMEMBER

Experience of joy I had in those seasons when life brought what I don't deserve.

*4 REPROCLAIM

Reproclaim involves positive, powerful confessions about you, your situation and future.

*REALITY

Then the reality of who you really are and what you should be begin to roll in.

HAPPINESS PROJECT

I have few suggestions for you today:

1. Take yourself out
2. Take someone you want to appreciate out on dinner or lunch.

DAY 7
LET GO

It hurts to let go, but sometimes it hurts more to hold on

Anonymous

You have come a long way on this journey of gratitude. Go ahead and complete it with a good finish.

Remember the wrongs of the past you have wished over and over to rewrite.

Remember that person you need to forgive and let off your mind.

Below are some quotes to ease your wounds.

"Cry. Forgive. Learn. Move on. Let your tears water the seeds of your future happiness."

– Steve Maraboli

"Let go. Why do you cling to pain? There is nothing you can do about the wrongs of yesterday. It is not yours to judge. Why hold on to the very thing which keeps you from hope and love?"

– Leo Buscaglia

"You can clutch the past so tightly to your chest that it leaves your arms too full to embrace the present."

– Jan Glidewe

DAY 7 HAPPINESS PROJECT

Write a letter, send text or gifts appreciate someone from your past that you didn't acknowledge at that time, maybe because of hurt or lack of opportunity.

Write a letter of forgiveness or reconciliation. Make peace with someone.

It will help to unload long-term burdens and sorrows.

DAY 8
DOCUMENT YOUR DISCOVERY

Get a new diary and write your discoveries from this experience

You never can tell, you may be writing your own book.

DAY 9
MY JOURNEY FROM GRATITUDE TO PURPOSE

Three years ago, I was dissatisfied with life, how things were not working as I planned for myself. I relocated to the UK after my internship as a young doctor. I had big dreams and vision of writing exams and start practice in the UK and start fulfilling my dreams. But things didn't play out as I planned. I began to ask God why? I needed answers? I was getting anxious and worried.

But things began to change as I sat down one day, and I said to myself, I am going to drop this fight for now and begin to appreciate what I do have now. Then I began to look inwards, then my passion to be a Coach, Mentor and Speaker began to emerge. I started taking steps towards developing my gifts and passion. Then I began to enjoy the blessedness of life,

I mentally brought myself into and swim in the goodness of life at the moment now,

How God blessed me with a wonderful husband and children, I began to appreciate and started telling people of how good God has taken care of me since childhood.

Of how I got favours that I don't deserve, people cheerfully blessed me with things they have turned other people down for, I mean countless blessings.

Then I discovered the three P'S that I discussed under the REPROCLAIM started happening. Perspective. Power, Positivity.

These 3P'S, I will also elaborate under the next system: PURPOSE & PASSION SYSTEM.

DAY 10
INTRODUCTIONS TO PURPOSE AND PASSION SYSTEM

P& P System would launch us into a new path. The discovery of your inner drive, to fuel your passion and at the end fulfils purpose.

There are a lot of unhappy people spending their time away from work escaping, complaining, or simply doing nothing instead of paying the price to change their circumstances.

There are so many in careers they don't enjoy or lack motivation for. They are longing to discover their hidden talents and gifts to lead them to fulfilment and purpose.

One of psychology's most steady findings {low self-awareness} is that people generally lack insight into their actual talents—they tend to think they're better than they really are.

While some blame others and situation for their unproductivity and unhappiness'.

In other words, few of us are willing to do what it takes to achieve what we desire.

HINDRANCE TO TAKING CHALLENGES

LOW SELF-ESTEEM

This is the horrible feeling of so many people:

I am not good enough

I am not smart enough

I am not good enough

My friends are better

I don't have many opportunities.

I'm just fine this way

It can't get any better

I NEVER GET TO FINISH WHAT I START

Kenny Akindele-Akande

This may be facts, but don't let this be your reality. Do not stop yourself. Give yourself this opportunity to explore happiness.

LOW SELF-AWARENESS

For some, it is lack of insight, knowledge of "job description". If you fall into this category, there is answer for you. Your problems are halfway solved. I have written this book for you, to give you the technical-know-how to finding your happiness.

PROCRASTINATION

Tomorrow	Someday,
In the future	sometimes
When I'm ready,	Another day
When I have everything	Whenever
Not yet,	perhaps.
Not sure,	

Does any or some of the above seem to be familiar with you? It is high time you changed them to the word "NOW".

COMFORT ZONE DILEMMA

A **comfort zone** is a psychological state in which things feel familiar to a person and they are at ease and in control of their environment, experiencing low levels of anxiety and stress.

Comfort zone is also behavioral space where your behaviors and performances fit a repetitive style and pattern that minimizes stress and risk.

It gives people a sense of MENTAL SECURITY.

A REDUCED STRESS LEVEL

LOW ANXIETY

ROUTINE HAPPINESS

A comfort zone is a beautiful place but nothing ever grows there

Annonymous

VENTURE OUT OF YOUR COMFORT ZONE

Everyone will at some point have this mental state but it is good to realise soon and get out of it. You will never know what joy or happiness that lies ahead until you get out.

A lot of people are afraid of feeling awkward, lonely or the uncertainty that surrounds venturing out.

YOUR LARGEST FEAR CARRIES YOUR GREATEST GROWTH

Annoymous

Give yourself that permission to find happiness, to discover your purpose and passion and pursue it.

That is what I want to help you with in this book. Let's go on and talk about the first P in Purpose & Passion System.

READ ON.

DAY 11
POTENTIALS

Not discovering your true potential is perhaps one of the bigger regrets, as people get older; realizing that you could've been more is one of the biggest emotional disturbances you can experience in your life.

Potential is having or showing capacity to develop into something in future.

Latent qualities or abilities that may be developed and lead to future success and usefulness.

Everybody has got a CREATIVE potential and from the MOMENT you can express this CREATIVE potential, you can start changing the world. Paulo Caulho

DISCOVER YOUR POTENTIALS

ICEBERG PRINCIPLE

An iceberg is a huge floating mass of ice detached from a glacier. Only the tip of the iceberg is seen but a large part is buried below water.

This principle expounded the fact that only ten per cent of an iceberg mass is seen outside while ninety per cent lies deep down in water.

I want to apply this principle in explaining our potential. I think it is sad to discover that the knowledge, skills and discovery we are using now are just 10% of the whole potential bank. 90% is still hidden or undiscovered.

That is to say what we exhibit now is not even all that is to us, that is amazing!

We all have potentials. All of us have within us nucleus of greatness. But everyone's potential is different. Some of us are great at telling stories; others excel at making scores, solving riddle and complex math problems, inventing things.

HOW TO DISCOVER YOUR POTENTIAL

OPEN MIND

Have an open mind, look inwards and not around. Your potentials are deep down in you.

FLEXIBILTY

Be flexible with the thoughts and ideas that come to your mind.

EXPLORE

Survey opportunities that are available for your potential in your environment.

DISCOVER

Discover your inner drive and passion

FUEL

Fuel your potential with passion

This will become clearer when you take the quiz in the happiness project for today.

DAY 11 HAPPINESS PROJECT

POTENTIAL AND PASSION QUIZ

These two-phenomenon work hand-in-hand. You can spell out your potential by what you are passionate about.

Your potential is what you are capable of doing or becoming; your innate abilities.

1. What are your gifts and
2. What are your talents?
3. What is your natural endowment?
4. What are you passionate about?
5. What can you do with little or no stress?
6. What do you enjoy doing?

Passion is a physical, emotional and spiritual fuel for your potential

Kenny Akindele-Akande

DAY 12
PREPARATION

Day 12 is preparation. Today, I want to show you how to give motion to your potentials. Remember, they are lying latent, they need a push.

QUATUM PHYSICS

POTENTIAL ENERGY VERSUS KINETIC ENERGY

In quantum physics, potential energy is described as the stored energy a body possess and this energy has the ability of being transformed into another kind of energy.

While Kinetic is the energy generated when a body is in motion.

That is to say that every latent potential has a stored up energy that can be transformed to into motion.

Therefore, set your Potential into Kinetic. So if you have discovered your potentials through the last happiness project quiz, it is time to set it/them in motion.

Set your latent qualities and abilities into motion.

Your latent potentials gradually atrophy if they are not exercised

Dr Max Hammer

B. HOW TO UNLOCK YOUR CREATIVE POTENTIALS

Look for every opportunity and platform to use your newly discovered potential. You have to use it, if not it can go back to latent.

C. PLAN

TOP 3 INTERESTS 1. 2. 3.	TOP 3 PASSIONS 1. 2. 3.	TOP 3 SKILLS 1. 2. 3.
TOP 3 PERSONAL QUALITIES 1. 2. 3.	TOP 3 TALENTS 1. 2. 3.	TOP 3 STRENGTHS 1. 2. 3.
WHAT IS YOUR PERSONALITY TYPE	WHAT IS YOUR TEMPARAMENT?	WHAT ARE YOUR DISLIKES?

KEYNOTES: STRENTH: developed talent PERSONALITY TYPES: Sanguine, TALENT: natural abilities Phlegmatic and Melancholic, Chloric

SKILL: learned abilities

D. EXECUTE

The amalgamation of all the criteria in the above table, can give you a reflection of what your potential and passion are.

That we eventually help you to know where to start from when you find out opportunities available for you.

KEEPING A PERSONAL DISCOVERY JOURNAL

If you are not sure of what some of this criteria are or you have not noticed them in yourself. You have to start paying close attention to yourself.

So at this point, it will be nice to keep a daily journal.

Journals provide that moment and place to jot down your

Talents

Passions.

Personal qualities

Strengths.

Journal is where you can collect and reflect privately on the likes and dislikes, to outline your discovery of yourself each day.

Anonymous

Writing down your thoughts and ideas ... your hopes and dreams .. helps you learn more about yourself than hours spent gazing into the mirror.

DAY 13

PURSUE

Now that you have discovered your potential and you have set it in motion. It is time to pursue.

To stay on track and get your happiness.

To Pursue is to follow and try to catch or capture (someone or something) for usually a long distance or time.

Pursue is not an aimless following, it is aimed at capturing no matter how far the distance.

So this is the part where I say, don't give up. It won't come easy; there would be opposition, a reminder of where you are coming from.

Don't worry, just keep moving!

3 STEPS TO PURSUE AND STAY ON COURSE

1. **GOALS**

   You must be clear about what you are running after and set goals you really want to achieve. Remember Happiness is what you want to achieve. How to set S.M.A.R.T Goals will be discussed in DAY 18.

2. **PLAN**

   Have an outlined step-by-step plan of how you are going to achieve your goal. Your plan is your roadmap to your desired destination.

3. **COMMITMENT**

   Before you start your pursuit of a goal, make a commitment to yourself that you will work toward it for a definite period of time and won't give up before that time arrives.

   Make this dated time as long or as short as you want but the important thing is not to quit before the apportioned time.

   When the target arrives, you can then decide whether to continue with the strategy you're currently following or make some changes to it.

Revise your strategies but don't quit. Quitting will only strengthen and accentuate your inability to persevere and see things through.

DAY 13 HAPPINESS PROJECT

STRATEGISE TO PURSUE

1. Write down your top 10 goals in their utmost priority.

2. Outline step-step plan to achieve them,

3. Write down your commitment to your plan.

4. Paste the paper in you room, above your dress mirror. Place it anywhere visible for you.

DAY 14
PERSEVERE

LET PERSEVERANCE BE YOUR ENGINE

AND HOPE YOUR FUEL

PERSEVERANCE

Now that we are clear about pursuing, that is to turn your potential and passion into energy that fuels your daily life. This will give you momentum achieve true happiness.

Perseverance is persistence and tenacity, the effort required to do something and keep doing it till the end, even if it's hard. **Perseverance** originally comes from the Latin perseverantia and **means** to abide by something strictly.

HOW TO PERSEVERE

1. **GET RID OF SELF-DOUBT**

    It's really difficult to make progress unless you believe you're capable of persevering. Stop comparing yourself with others.

2. **IDENTIFY OBSTACLES**

    Identify potential obstacles you could face along the way to discovery. This will not only prepare you mentally for when you do come across them, but it will also help you in the process of devising alternative strategies and eventuality plans.

3. **SEEK HELP**

    Seek out help and moral support from family and friends or mentors. They will help keep you to stay focused and motivated on following through until you achieve your goal.

4. SELF-CONTROL

Self-control is a must when developing perseverance in daily life. Exercising self-control ensures you remain focused on the task: deriving happiness and joy and distracted.

5. DAILY HABITS

Establish consistent daily habits and rituals.

Keep your mind and body healthy.

Taking daily measures to stay healthy will go a long way toward helping you persevere.

Here are a few tips to staying healthy

- Eat a wholesome diet. Make sure you're getting plenty of nutritious, vegetables and fruits.

- Eat whole grains, meat, and healthy fats..

- Get plenty of sleep. A full night's sleep can make the difference between having a bad day and a great one.

- Get 7 to 8 hours nightly whenever possible.

- Regular exercise: like walking, yoga, running, biking, swimming, or another activity, move around as much as you can. Exercise puts you in a good mood and keeps you in shape for whatever life may throw at you. Trying a regimen of exercising for 30 minutes daily is a great place to start. Take small steps of progress steadily everyday will mean that your efforts will compound and success will be inevitable.

6. Cultivate your spirituality

Many people find that grooming a sense of being part of something bigger is comforting and energizing. Having a spiritual life can help you find your purpose again when you don't know where to turn.

- If you're religious, attend services regularly. If you pray, do it often.

- Practice meditation and other forms of spiritual awareness.

- Spend time in natural places, and appreciate the blessing the universe, of forests, oceans, rivers and open sky.

The importance of perseverance in life cannot be overemphasised.

To achieve any notable goal or success then you must have the stamina to stay the distance.

If perseverance is something you lack then by following the tips above and applying a smallest amount of effort you will soon realize that nothing is beyond your reach.

CELEBRATE YOUR ACCOMPLISHMENT

Appreciate and celebrate your gradual success. Evaluate yourself and see how far you have come. Buy yourself a drink, congratulate yourself, and take yourself out on a date. YOU ARE THE BEST!

If you have trouble feeling proud of your own accomplishments, try writing yourself a letter as if you were writing to a friend. Imagine that your friend has been doing the work that you have. You would feel proud of him, right? You'd probably encourage her to keep going and tell her what great work she's doing. Why would you treat yourself with any less kindness?

DAY 14 HAPPINESS PROJECT

1. Write down a list of perceived opposition or hindrance to your goal.

2. Deduce daily habits that can help you overcome them

3. Write down your personal spiritual activities you can cultivate to help you persevere.

4. Seek out one or two friends or family member that can motivate and always challenge you to go.

5. Lastly, seek out support network in your community.

DAY 15

POWER

Coming through this journey, you'd perceive you are beginning to take charge of your life, take control of your thoughts and redirect your emotions to produce positive energy to drive your life. You now have the power to achieve greatness.

And achievement is something accomplished, especially by superior ability, special effort, great courage, a great or heroic deed. Synonyms: attainment, realization, accomplishment, fulfilment, implementation, execution, performance.

Achievement brings happiness

Happiness lies in the joy of achievement and the thrill of creative effort.
-Franklin D. Roosevelt

Happiness does not come from doing easy work but from the afterglow of satisfaction that comes from the achievement of a difficult task that demanded our best.
-Theodore Issac Rubin

Great achievement is usually born of great sacrifice, and never the result of selfishness.

-Napoleon Hill

Happiness is found through working hard and achieving progress.

PERSONAL ACHIEVEMENT

You have achieved this power and success yourself. This personal achievement will

1. *Boost your confidence and places you in a higher orbit.*
2. *Help you experience a new perspective to life*
3. *Power you into the next level in your life*
4. *Lastly, it will bring forth the NEW YOU into existence*

YOU ARE NEVER A MISTAKE

YOU WERE BORN FOR A PURPOSE

NEVER UNDERESTIMATE YOUR POTENTIAL

NEVER UNDERMINE YOUR OWN STRENGTH

YOU ARE CREATED TO BE GREAT

Kenny Akindele-Akande

DAY 15 HAPPINESS PROJECT

MIRROR MANIFESTO

"The power to shape your reality lies within you, therefore the most important voice you will ever hear is your own."

- Max Patrick

Go in front of your mirror

Look into the eyes of that person you see in the mirror

Do you love what you see?

Make the following confessions to that image

I WILL WIN

The power is within me

The answer is in me

I am the answer to all my searches

I am the goal

I am the prize

I am worth it

I have the potential

I will develop my gift

I will pursue my dreams

I will persevere

I will be great

I WILL WIN

Kenny Akindele-Akande

DAY 16
REVISION OF PURPOSE &
PASSION SYSTEM

POTENTIAL

Your potential is what you are capable of doing or becoming, your innate abilities.

1. What are your gifts and
2. What are your talents?
3. What is your natural endowment?
4. What are you passionate about?
5. What can you do with little or no stress?
6. What do you enjoy doing?

PREPARATION

Prepare to give motion to your potentials. Remember, they are lying latent, they need a push. Look for every opportunity and platform to use your newly discovered potential. You have to use it, if not it can go back to latent.

PURSUE

This is the part where I say, get ready to pursue, get ready to fight for what you believe in. Go get your happiness.

PERSERANCE

Perseverance is persistence and tenacity, the effort required to do something and keep doing it till the end, even if it's hard. Persevere, keep pushing, don't give in or give up.

POWER

Happiness is found through working hard and achieving progress. Your achievement is your power, your story and your medal.

DAY 17
HAPPINESS PROJECT

Now let's acknowledge the list you made in DAY 11 Happiness project.

Your interest, passion, potential and strength, skills etc.

PLAN

TOP 3 INTERESTS 1. 2. 3.	TOP 3 PASSIONS 1. 2. 3.	TOP 3 SKILLS 1. 2. 3.
TOP 3 PERSONAL QUALITIES 1. 2. 3.	TOP 3 TALENTS 1. 2. 3.	TOP 3 STRENGTHS 1. 2. 3.
WHAT IS YOUR PERSONALITY TYPE	WHAT IS YOUR TEMPARAMENT?	WHAT ARE YOUR DISLIKES?

Work through this list table again; make a list of your discoveries. You will need this tomorrow DAY 18.

DAY 18
HOW DO YOU PREPARE

I have to congratulate you at this point; you have made a commendable progress. I mean, we are in Day 18.

You have come through Gratitude system, to discovering your purpose, now you need to prepare how to pursue your purpose so that to have fulfilment and happiness in life.

Now, you know what you want and you are ready to fight for it.

You have discovered your purpose and it's worth pursuing.

SATISFACTION AND CONTENTMENT

Before you go on to prepare, you have to understand the following facts:

1. Purpose brings a sense of fulfilment and satisfaction.

2. Satisfaction in who you are, in becoming YOU brings happiness.

3. It is high time you stopped beating yourself over and over again for the mistake and failures of the past.

4. It's a new dawn; it's a new day.

5. A new life is unfolding for you right now, so BE HAPPY.

SET GOALS

The first rule of goal setting is, talk about goal setting. Tell everyone who cares to listen what your goals are and your new path to finding happiness. The extra pressure will stimulate you to act upon your words.

HAPPY LIVING S.M.A.R.T GOALS

Specific: HAPPINESS

Measurable: STEADY GROWTH

Achievable: PASSION

Relevant: PURPOSE

Time-bound: 30 DAYS

Specific

Happiness is your specification for this journey. To find happiness is your goal.

Measurable

Your steady growth in gratitude and discovering of who you are will be your measurement for this progress.

Achievable

Always refill your fuel tank for this journey. The fuel is your PASSION.

Relevant

This pursuit is about discovering purpose, the reason why you exist. Fulfilling your purpose is relevant to happy living.

Time-bound

30-Day journey to finding happiness. And after the 30 days, you continue living the rest of your life in TRUE HAPPINESS.

HAPPY LIVING SUPPORT AND NETWORKING.

Who knows, you may be helping someone link the missing bits in their journey too or better still you find someone who wants to do the same but needs support. The more people you speak to, the better chance you'll have of meeting individuals you can cooperate with and achieve your outcome

DAY 19
SET OUT TO PURSUE

On your mark……..Get set….GO

As the eyes of a runner is set on the go, the end, which is winning the race, your focus needs to be on the finish line.

There is nothing stopping you now.

THE END IN VIEW

One of the best ways to stay motivated is by visualising the change you want to see. Make this image clear in your mind - the 'you' in X amount of weeks time - so when the odd setback does happen, you won't be fazed and will come back stronger than ever.

And when you do hit your target, treat yourself; you deserve it.

DAY 20
INTRODUCTION TO LIVE LARGE STRATEGY

7 L'S TO LIVING LARGE

Living large strategy will teach you how to live larger than life.

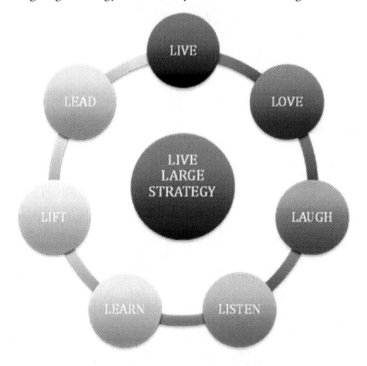

As against the general saying live large to mean indulge freely in luxury or luxuries. With Live large strategy, I want to expound to you {7L'S 1. Live 2. Love 3. Laugh 4. Listen 5. Learn 6. Lift 7. Lead} to finding happiness and contentment in living a purpose driven life.

You have discovered purpose; Living large strategy will teach you how to stay on purpose and on top of your game in life.

DAY 21
LIVE

MOMENT
MAXIMIZE
MAKE

MOMENT

PRESENT/PAST/FUTURE DILEMMA

We're like icebergs. Two-thirds of our enormity is hidden under the surface. What if we flipped it so our enormity could be seen? And acknowledged. And shared.

- No one cares or sees the big chunk of ice beneath the iceberg
- We only see and appreciate the iceberg
- Success is good but it does not lead to happiness.

If not why will some so called successful and wealthy people end up empty and unhappy?

- Live every moment
- Let every moment count

- Why live life like you would have a second chance to come to life again
- Live every second and minutes as if it would be your last
- Live Light: Don't carry WORRY

WHAT WILL YOU DO IF YOU ARE TOLD YOU HAVE FEW MORE DAYS TO LIVE?

I read a story of a man {stage name George} diagnosed with a terminal illness and giving few 30 days to live.

His doctor brought his test results and scans and treatment options {not that he has any option} on his hospital bed. As the doctor narrated his ordeal and medical jargons, George watched his life live a video clip fading off before his very own eyes like a vapour.

He thought of how he had fought, won, failed, passed, he thought of friends and families and every relationships he has made. He cried and wailed more for his regrets, what he would regret when he dies.

He was also given a clinical psychologist to help him through his last day's journey.

The psychologist first question to him was, if you were to come back to life or giving a second chance to live, what will you do? How will you improve some aspects of your life?

He gave George time to think and paper to write and plan his second coming.

SECOND CHANCE JOURNAL

He resolute to rewrite all his wrongs with each of the subtitles below:

1. RELATIONSHIP
2. CAREER
3. FINANCE
4. PASSIONS

RELATIONSHIP

George has not been in good terms with his mother because she lied about who his father was for 20 years. He was only getting to know who is true father was some months ago and unfortunately the man died some months before, this heightened his pain and anger toward his mum more. He never had the opportunity to know and share time with his true father.

He then could understand how his stepfather {the one he believed was his father} was cruel to him when he was growing up.

He has always asked his mother why he was been maltreated amidst other children.

So he resulted to first forgive and draw his mother closer.

Meanwhile some 5 years before then George had an affair with a lady he was not intending getting married to, she got pregnant in the process but George blatantly refused to accept responsibility for the child.

So for five years he had a child out there, living without his true father, probably the lady is married to another man, and George's child his calling another man dad.

It dawn on George, that his story looked like history wants to repeat itself.

Right there, he planned to find his ex-girlfriend and son.

CAREER

As touching career, He is a clerk in a hospital. He had wanted to be a paramedic, but never had the chance. So he started reading online and looking out for how to read a course on paramedics.

FINANCE

George was in a bad shape financially; he gambles with his money a lot. Right there he pledged to stop gambling and started seeking help to break free and that addiction.

PASSION

His passion and heart have always gone to the aged. He goes to old people's home regularly before he fell ill. So he decided to raise awareness and funds for the aged homes in his community. Then signed a declaration after a long list of resolution, it goes thus.

DECLARATION

Then, George declared, if I am giving another opportunity to live:

I would do the above and live life to the maximum.

His psychologist broke down his resolution into a 30-day journey; he has one objective to carry out in a day.

On his 30 day journey, as he reconciled with his mum and ex lover and finally met his son, he began to feel less ill and his condition began to get better.

After 30 days, he was bright and better. As a matter of fact, he has not felt ill for days. Since he was told 30 days to live, he was preparing to say goodbye to the world.

All of a sudden, his doctor dashed into his hospital suite and a pleaded for an immediate scan and check-up on him. Only to discover his illness was not terminal after all. His case file and scan had been mistakenly swapped with another patient who has the same name and initials with him.

The doctors and the hospital were pleading that he should not sue them that they can compensate, that he has a right to be furious.

He was quiet for a while, bubbled with mixed feeling, at the end, he express his discovering. Everyone expected him to be angry. Like he does have every right to. To their amazement, he said "Thank you for helping me LIVE"

Thank you for helping find my LIFE back

Thank you for giving me HAPPINESS"

You have given me another perspective to live and another shot to live a good life.

So he left the hospital happy, ready to maximize his new life.

MAXIMIZE

It is time to live life to the maximum.

- Maximize every opportunity that comes your way
- Make wise use of relationships you have
- Your gifts and Talents sometimes open the doors that skill or profession can't
- Use your brain, mind and intellect

MAKE

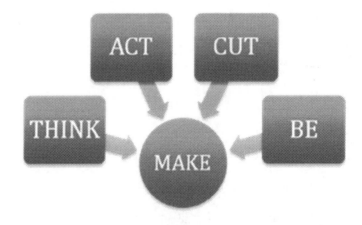

BE CREATIVE

We are not properly born with creativity but we can build and cultivate it, it is a skill we can acquire. You never can tell what more you can do or become until you start making something.

Creative People are curious, flexible, persistent and independent with a tremendous spirit of love and adventure
Anonymous

THINK

Think and reflect on new ideas and concepts. Practice openness, keep asking question.

ACT

It is time to act differently

Seek out unexpected experiences if you wish to think differently and so approach problems with a fresh perspective.

CUT

Cut every distraction that can hinder your creative thinking. Neuroscientists claimed those moments of insight and excitement leads to increase in brain energy waves within the brain. Therefore, happy moments and creativity can work hand-in hand. When we are in a happy state, we tend to be swift to think and act promptly.

BE

Let all these new discovering of the new you become a lifestyle. Cultivate a lifestyle of happiness. Always work towards creating that happy state to stimulate creativity.

Most people tend to look at those people who develop creative ideas consistently with a kind of reverence. And people who do seem blessed with a talent for creativity live in fear that talent will run out some day and they will be just like everybody else.

Anonymous

DAY 22
LOVE

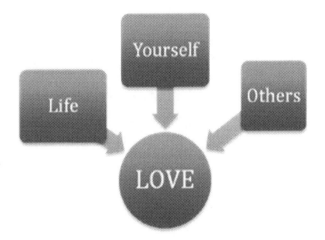

Love LIFE

Love YOURSELF

Love OTHERS

LIFE

NATURE/UNIVERSE

- Nature is an equal gift to everyone
- Take time out to appreciate the beauty of Nature.
- The seas, the climate, mountains and hill. Time and Season seem to be well planned.
- There is surely a brilliant brain behind their daily functions.

Love is a powerful force; it is the force behind life, nature and the universe

Kenny Akindele-Akande

Love YOURSELF

I Love my life

I love my heart.

I love my body

I love my mind.

I love my home

I love my family.

I am highly inspired

I am full of energy

I am well and healthy

I am physically, emotional and spiritual fit

I feel vibrant

I love to sing

I love to dance

I love to dance

I love to learn

I love to listen

I LOVE ME

Kenny Akindele-Akande

FALL IN LOVE WITH YOURSELF.

- Fall in love with your future

- Start loving your journey

- Date yourself

- Take yourself out, Give yourself a treat

- Life is too short to miss out on these

- When will you stop loving to be like other people

BE YOURSELF

BE YOURSELF

ACCEPT YOURSELF

ENDORSE YOURSELF

BLESS YOURSELF

TRUST YOURSELF

EXPRESS YOURSELF

FORGIVE YOURSELF

HELP YOURSELF

BE KIND TO YOURSELF

BE HAPPY WITH YOURSELF

BE YOURSELF

Kenny Akindele-Akindele

LOVE OTHERS

Share enormously.

Laugh enormously.

Create enormously.

Act enormously.

Anonymous

EXPAND YOUR HEART

The heart has been used in expression of some common idioms like "from the bottom of my heart", "young at heart" and "with all my heart". Heart is the centre of our lives. The focus of all emotions. Therefore I can say, "Expand your heart"! In understanding life, others and situations, you need to be able to view and accommodate changes. We cannot be in control of how people relate to us or how situation will turn out but we can change how we react.

No matter what life throws at you or do to you, let your hear develop and build the capacity to stay above. Kenny Akindele-Akande

FORGIVE...LET IT GO

Give your weight to the waters.... Kenny Akindele-Akande

It's like when you are learning to swim for the first time, the first basic lesson is to give your weight to the water, let the water carry you and feel safe in the arms of the waves. That is the lesson forgiveness teaches in life. You can't enjoy a healthy life and harbour hurts inside.

Another lesson forgiveness teaches is when you forgive people especially when they don't deserve it, you are staying on top of your game. That is what this book is about.

PRINCIPLE OF BOUYANCY

An object will float if the gravitational (downward) force is less than the buoyancy (upward) force. So, in other words, an object will float if it weighs less than the amount of water it displaces. This explains why a rock will sink while a huge **boat** will float. The rock is heavy, but it displaces only a little water.

BOUYANCY FORCE VERSUS GRAVITATIONAL FORCE

Buoyancy force is the upward force that resists the gravitational force that tends to pull every object downwards.

Boats stay afloat with heavy loads because they're hollow; they aren't solid...

If you want to stay above the turbulence of life, you have to stay light...be determined to resist the gravitational pull of hurt that may want to pull you down. Let the buoyant force of forgiveness keeps you up at all time.

FORGIVENESS USES THE PRINCIPLE OF BOUYANCY

Forgiveness is the conscious, considered action determined to relieve the person who has hurt us of their due punishment. It is divine, "to forgive is divine". True forgiveness requires love, strength of character and patience. Forgiveness helps you void your heart of hatred, grudges and blames.

Forgive yourself,

Forgive others,

Forgive situations.

Let go of the hurts

Let go of the pain

Let go of the blame.

You deserve a second chance. Kenny Akindele-Akindele

Learn to forgive, for it is sublime: learn to love, for it is divine.

G. de Purucke

DAY 23
LAUGHS

FACTS ABOUT LAUGHTER

- Laughter is a profound and recognised antidote to stress, pain, and conflict.
- A hearty and good laughter works faster than any medicine.
- Science claims that laughter is the best medicine
- Laughter is contagious

We will be considering laughter under three points

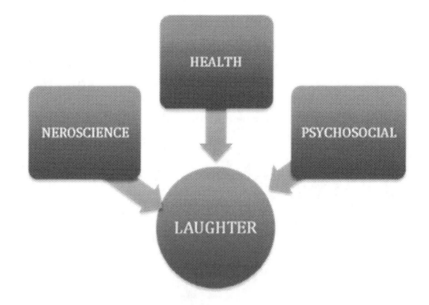

1. **NEUROSCIENCE OF LAUGHTER**
2. **HEALTH BENEFITS OF LAUGHTER**
3. **PSYCHOSOCIAL PERSPECTIVE TO LAUGHTER**

FREUD'S RELIEF THEORY

Relieve theory is one of the three classification of humour associated with Sigmund Freud and Herbert Spencer. They both concluded that humour is a way of releasing saved nervous energy. It states that laughing- generating circumstances are pleasant because they produce psychic energy.

APPLICATION OF FREUD'S RELIEF THEORY IN COMEDY

Freud believes that jokes are more than what they seem. When one is faced with situation that creates tension within, jokes and humour release laughter, which is able to cleanse their system of built-up tension and absurdity.

IN MOVIES

The relief theory is also being applied in plays and movies we watch. Especially, the thriller and comic relief. It is a technique used to diffuse the high-tension built-up when people are watching a particular movie

1. NEUROSCIENCE OF LAUGHTER

Scott has also discovered that different kinds of laughter activate different areas of the brain. "People automatically classify heard laughter -- which means, no matter what, that laughter is always meaningful. **Sophie Scott.**

Happy Chemicals released when we laugh.

There are four major chemicals in the brain that influence our happiness (DOSE):

1. Endorphins.
2. Dopamine
3. Oxytocin
4. Serotonin

A. ENDORPHINS AND EUPHORA

Research on brain and moods show that when the body comes under stress or pain, neurochemicals called endorphins are produced in the brain's hypothalamus and pituitary gland. Endorphins are known to be structurally similar to the drug morphine, are considered natural painkillers because they activate opioid receptors in the brain that help reduce discomfort.

They also help bring about feelings of euphoria and general well being. "Endorphins are also involved in natural reward system related to activities such as exercise, feeding, drinking, maternal attachment and maternal sexual activity.

B. **DOPAMINE AND MOTIVATION**

Dopamine helps us release the energy we need to get the rewards we want. Dopamine motivates you to take action toward your goals and gives you a surge of reinforcing pleasure when achieving them. Procrastination, self-doubt, and lack of enthusiasm are linked with low levels of dopamine.

C. **SEROTONIN AND SAFETY**

Serotonin is the chemical responsible for the feeling of superiority to others. It was discovered in mammals, that serotonin is released when it sees that he is superior or bigger than another. This is as result makes the mammal feel safe and respected. Some researchers also regard serotonin as a chemical that is responsible for maintaining mood balance, and that a deficit of serotonin leads to depression. Drop in the level of secretion of serotonin has also been related to lack of sexual intimacy. It is popularly thought to be a contributor to feelings of well-being and happiness

D. **OXYTOCIN AND BONDING**

Oxytocin is a hormone that plays a significant role in bonding friendships, families, marriages and most importantly **maternal instinct**. It is produced by hypothalamus and secreted by pituitary. **It is referred to as "love hormone". It helps us to love, trust and feel a sense of belonging.**

APPLICATION OF HAPPY CHEMICALS

With the right amount and balance of these chemicals, you can to push through pain and promote wellbeing. A genuine belly laughs will 'juddering up' your insides in a good way. Genuine laughing is thought to relief fear.

2. HEALH BENEFITS OF LAUGHTER

MENTAL

PHYSICAL

MENTAL

- Add joy and zest to life
- Eases anxiety and tension
- Relieves stress
- Improves mood
- Strengthens resilience
- **Laughter stops distressing emotions**
- **Laughter helps you relax and recharge** and restore, rejuvenate
- **Laughter shifts perspective**
- **Laughter draws you closer to others**

PHYSICAL

- **Laughter protects the heart.**
- **Laughter burns calories.**
- Relaxes muscles
- Decreases pain
- Lowers stress hormones
- Boost immunity
- **Laughter triggers the release of endorphins**
- **Laughter lightens anger's heavy load**

3. PSYCHOSOCIAL

Laughter is an amazing strategy for people to feel good together.

Sophie Scott.

- Bonding: Promotes healthy bonding
- Law of attraction: attracts others to us
- Enhances teamwork
- It helps diffuse conflict
- It's contagious, spreads to the other person

LAUGHTER IS CONTAGIOUS

Can you explain why you suddenly burst into laughter just by seeing someone laugh? This can attest to laughter being contagious. Laughter is under marginal mindful control; it is spontaneous and relatively unrestricted. It shows that Laughter is infectious and can spread from one person to another like contagious infection. Contagious laughter is a captivating display of Homo sapiens, a social mammal.

LAUGH

    LAUGH

        LAUGH

            LAUGH

                LAUGH

                    LAUGH

DAY 24
LISTEN

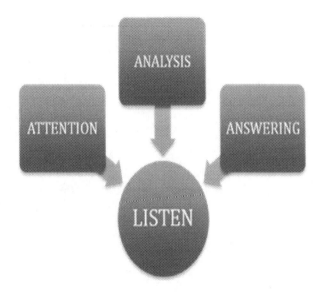

In our day-to-day life, listening play a key role.

Listen in such a way that others love to talk to you.

Speak in such a way that others tend to listen to you

Anonymous

LISTENING IS AN ART

THAT REQUIRES ATTENTION

OVER TALENT,

SPIRIT OVER EGO

OTHERS OVER SELF

Dean Jackson

1. ATTENTION

The greatest act of love is paying attention.

Diane Sawyer

Pay Attention, Analyse the information presented, and then give an intelligent Answer.

Kenny Akindele-Akande

In counselling and psychology, the art of listening is key. Paying attention requires active participation. This means not just listening to what people say but taking an interest in them, making sure they are comfortable with coming clean without been judged. This skill is important in relationships, workplace and community.

2. ANALYSE

Examine the information given in detail, without attaching emotions or personal experience before you provide answer. Don't rush to answer, in some cases you don't have to answer immediately. Don't jump to conclusion.

3. ANSWER

Giving a profound intelligent answer is the next quality. With an act of love and calm disposure, give answer; reassure love if it is the case that needs it. Make sure the answer you provided is the best available for that situation.

HOW TO BE AN EFFECTIVE LISTENER

LISTEN TO YOUR SPIRIT

It is a universal knowledge that man is a spirit being. If not why do we die? Or what happens when a man dies? In Christian theology, the **tripartite** view of man holds that man is a composite of three distinct components:

Body, Soul and Spirit.

The Spirit is the inner core of man, the most powerful force in creation and stronger than anything than may happen to it.

Conscience is another interesting phenomenon in man; it is the spiritual and supernatural principle in man.

God, the universe or the supernatural always speaks to man through their spirit and conscience.

Do not fight your conscience or spirit when they are integrating wisdom into you, many people had lost their lives or wealth when they ignored the warnings of these two powerful forces.

They come back to regret and lament "If I had known better, I would have listen to my conscience".

Before you make a decision, always search your spirit and meditate on the consequences of your actions after.

LISTEN TO OTHERS

Listening is an art; a highway to other people's heart and it requires patience. Listening is a skill we need to learn in order to evolve as a person and unleash our potential. It also helps us to become effective in communication.

When you listen to others more, you tend to gain more. It is true that they enjoy an undivided and non-judgmental attention from you but you gradually grow in patience and compassion towards people. You begin to understand people and life more, you become someone who magically finds solution to people's puzzle just by the act of listening. People feel valued, esteemed and respected when their friends and family listen to them.

DAY 24 HAPPINESS PROJECT

S.W.O.T ANALYSIS

In today's project, we will be analysing behaviours and complains in relationships and family. Let's consider couple in a marriage.

Lying behind most complains of a partner in marriage is a bowel of love, though they may sound frustrated and not capable of passing across their message, but the truth is they still love their partner and they want him or her to change. They probably hate the situation and not the partner.

The mixed emotions, anger-love sometimes leads to disaster. However, the ability to discern, analyse and see past what people say or how they act is imperative.

In most organisations, SWOT analysis is often conducted as a major part of a situation analysis.

SWOT is an acronym that refers to strengths, weaknesses, opportunities and threats.

The way we talk or respond to situation is the combination of these qualities in varying degree.

STRENGTHS

WEAKNESSES

OPPORTUNITIES

THREATS

For example, an insecure man who is afraid of another man taking his woman and therefore acts in an overprotective manner with his wife is an indication of THREAT.

The degree of threat and weakness had overpowered other SWOT qualities.

His weakness

For some reasons of low self-esteem, failure or not a feeling "not man enough".

His Threats

This weakness had created a leak in him, lack of confidence that led to other men being a

Threat to him.

PRACTICAL

I want to give you the opportunity to SWOT ANALYSE YOURSELF AND PEOPLE IN YOUR life.

After this analysis, what you discover can be shocking.

You may even realise that friends or family that you thought don't like you or always complain are not rude after all. Maybe they are trying to communicate something or maybe they are damaged inside and felt threatened.

The lesson today is to try to see past what people say or how they act. Then you will be able to answer in the correct perspective.

DAY 25
LEARN

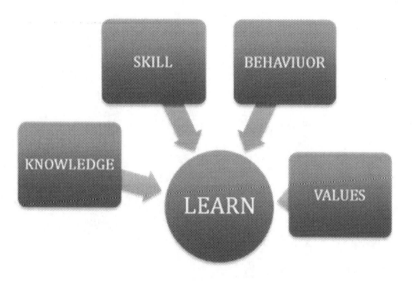

Learning is an integral part of life. We learn everyday, in every way at anytime either consciously or unconsciously.

There is self-assertion and satisfaction learning can bring to us. I will be showing the aspects of learning that can bring happiness to our lives.

KNOWLEDGE

Knowledge is power is one of the most popular quote of our time. Ages ago when knowledge was confined to the walls of school and pages of books, people can claim they could not access knowledge due to lack of money, distance or lack of education.

That is not the case in our modern world, people who can't read or write can access knowledge just by listening or watching because technology has over simplify life for us.

Even at that, so many still find it difficult to acquire knowledge. Knowledge is displayed through Internet that many of us can't but visit in a day. But we would rather laugh at jokes on social media, like or share information without actually learning.

Knowledge is power and when you applied that power into your life is called wisdom. You become king over those who don't have that knowledge; you may even become an authority in that field.

Knowledge **educates**

Knowledge elevates

Knowledge sets you apart

Knowledge makes you shine

Knowledge rewards

Knowledge blesses

Knowledge satisfies

Knowledge can bring happiness

Kenny Akindele-Akande

SET DAILY GOAL TO LEARN

Make a decision to acquire knowledge, set a daily target to learn something new that will help any aspect of your life.

KNOWLEDGE SOLVES PROBLEM

In life, challenges and problem are inevitable. You will persistently face problems every day, sometimes problems that you can't possibly seem to overcome. With knowledge, you can expand your abilities of thinking diagnostically and provide solutions to problem.

KNOWLEDGE HELPS SELF-DISCOVERY

Do you know that knowledge can actually make you realise who you truly are, when you begin to really think about and understand yourself. This alone can bring happiness.

Knowledge can help you in also discovering what makes you happy, what do you enjoy exploring and learning about?

SKILL

Skill defined by business dictionary as the ability and capacity acquired through deliberate, systematic, and sustained effort to smoothly and adaptively carryout complex activities or job functions involving ideas {cognitive skills} things {technical skills}, and /or people {interpersonal skills}.

Three significant features of this definition are:

1. Cognitive
2. Technical
3. Interpersonal

Cognitive skills

Cognitive abilities are brain-based skills we use to carry out any task from the simplest to the most complex. They have more to do with the mechanisms of how we learn, remember, problem-solve, and pay attention, rather than with any actual knowledge.

When you master and cultivate habits that develop your cognitive skills, you tend to be more happy and proud of yourself and vice versa.

Habits that improves Cognitive Function

1. Optimism
2. Openness
3. Physical Activities
4. Creativity
5. Social Network
6. Meditation
7. Games
8. Restful Sleep

Happy people are more creative, solve problems faster, and tend to be more mentally alert. Susan Reynolds

Technical Skill

Even though soft skill {such as good communication, teamwork, and interpersonal relationships} may have overshadowed technical {hard} skill in this time and age, the place of technical skill cannot be undermined in our workplaces.

Many people seeking employment ignorantly play down on technical skills because of their sound soft skill. It is good to find a balance of the two in order to be effective.

Technical skill include the specific knowledge and abilities required for success in a job, which can be **computer skill, web design, proficiency in a foreign language, typing speed, nursing, finance, electrical, accounting, finance, writing, mathematics, legal skills, etc**.

Even if you don't require any of this in your job description, you will need some skill in your day-to-day life.

Interpersonal skills

People who have high interaction skill with others always win with people. Interpersonal skills are the life skills we use everyday when we communicate and interact with other people, either as individual or groups.

It is not limited to workplaces; it can be applied in relationships and family life.

Key interpersonal skills you need:

Develop the ability to relate to others

Be patience with other

Be an active listener

Have good communication skills

Develop an ability to trust

Know when and how to show empathy.

With an effective interpersonal skill, both you and the individual or people you are relating with live "happily ever after".

VALUE

A value system is a set of principles or ideals that drive and guide your behaviour. Your value system gives you structure and purpose by helping you determine what is meaningful and important to you.

Benefits of having a good value system

1. Integrity: It helps you express what you truly are and what you stand for.
2. Character: It defines your character and impacts on your way of life.
3. Decision making: you make good and responsible decisions in life.

BEHAVIOUR

Behaviour is essential as it shapes our character and personality.

It helps us in building a good charisma. Good behaviour is one quality that can throw us in the good light no matter what position we hold in the society or how poor or rich we are.

Benefits of good behaviour

1. You become a better person yourself.
2. You become a reference point for others
3. It helps you withstand the storms of life.
4. It stabilises you and help you derive fulfilment.

Conscious effort at projecting good behaviour is a winning attitude.

Kenny Akindele-Akande

HAPPINESS PROJECT

MAKE A LIST OF THE FOLLOWING

1. Write Top 5 Knowledge you desire to acquire
2. Write down Top 5 skills you had long to learn along time ago.
3. List down your values
4. Evaluate your value system

DAY 25
LIFT

LAW OF LIFT/AERODYNAMICS

An airfoil generates **lift** by exerting a downward force on the air as it flows past.

NEWTON'S LAW OF MOTION

According to Newton's third Law, air must exert an equal but opposite (upward) force on the airfoil, which is the **lift**.

The flow is turned in one direction, and the **lift** is generated in the opposite direction, according to Newton's Third **Law** of action and reaction are equal but opposite.

LIFE'S WEIGHT AND CHALLENGES

Life is full of challenges, problems and weight that will threaten to swallow us up, but we have a choice, to choose how to react.

The only way to react to life's situation is not to allow it swallow us up, but we have to try and launch a counteract equal but opposite force, following Newton's law of motion.

If you want to go up and stay on top {ever lifted}, this counteracting force has to be stronger. This counteract force **is FORCE OF LIFT**.

It must be stronger than the FORCE OF WEIGHT that wants to weigh you down.

LIFT YOURSELF

If you watch depressed and hurting people closely, they have a falsified humbly demeanour, they can barely look up or enjoy life. They are coiled up in their situation and can't open up to love from nature and others.

Lifting yourself with a strategize force of lift comes from how you deal with situations everyday, betrayal and hurt from loved ones.

And how to go on from there.

WHAT you tell YOURSELF

Everyday

Will either lift YOU UP

Or

Tear YOU DOWN.

Anonymous

LIFT OTHERS

LAW OF AERODYNAMICS

We rise when we lift others

Kenny Akindele-Akande

Lift is the force that acts in an upward direction to support the aircraft in the air.

It counteracts the effect of weight. Lift must be greater than or equal to the weight if flight is to be sustained.

It is much easier to lift others when you are up. Lift yourself above life's worries, you never know, you may be opportune to lift others in future.

I have not seen an aircraft or lift that tries to lift people that remain on the ground itself.

When you lift others, you will be rising yourself.

Therefore, in this pursuit of happiness, lift others into happiness.

GIVE A HELPING HAND

Help others, no matter how little. You may think it is nothing, but to that person you are helping, it is just enough.

ENCOURAGE OTHERS

Be the listening ears, pay attention to someone. Say nice and positive words to people.

Don't flatter but be sincere.

Leave people better than you met them. Anonymous

DAY 26
LEAD

YOURSELF

Now that you have come from gratitude, to discovering purpose and now living large, you need to stay strong and be on top of your game always.

Let's be sure you Know Yourself

You can't lead someone you can't recognize. Hence, start finding yourself and knowing whom you really are. You can achieve it by spending some quiet time alone, reflecting with your past experiences, lessons and realizations.

TEN STEPS TO LEADING YOURSELF

1. Be in charge of your life

    You are in charge of your happiness now.

2. Motivate yourself

    In leading yourself, you have to learn how to sacrifice your own comfort to consistently motivate yourself.

3. **Have a positive outlook to life**

    It is important that from this time forward, you have to shun negativity. Ignore any memories or present situation that draws you back into negativity.

4. **Have a good spirit**

    Be happy, be cheerful and have a positive outlook to the future.

5. **Seek harmony in your inner self**

    Forgive yourself and others of the past. Hold no grudge against anyone. Be free as a bird.

6. **Be Inspired**

Inspiration is based on one's passion. Through this journey, you must have discovered your passion and purpose. If not still take time out to meditate and find them. Find the things you love to do and start doing them naturally and blissfully.

7. **Honesty**

Honesty is the best policy, they say. Be honest with yourself and others. Don't live double-life, let people know you for who you are?

8. **Trust yourself**

Be your first fan, your best cheerleader. No one can trust you as you will trust yourself if you truly know yourself.

9. **Be confident**

Self-confidence is the first mandatory requirement for any endeavour. Accept who you are, aspire to be the best, when you fall, rise up again and pursue your happiness.

10. **DON'T GIVE UP on your pursuit of your happiness**

DAY 27
ATTITUDE

You cannot control what happens to you, but you can control your ATTITUDE toward what happens to you, and in that, you will be mastering change rather than allowing it to master you.

Brian Tracy

Happiness does not depend on any external condition; it is governed by our mental ATTITUDE.

Dale Carnegie

It is your ATTITUDE not your aptitude, that determines your altitude.

Zig Ziglar

A bad attitude is like a flat tyre, if you don't change it, you are going nowhere.

Dailykarmaquotes.com

DAY 28
CHOICES

Life is a matter of CHOICES, and every choice you make makes you.

John c. Maxwell

Life is about CHOICES, some we regret, some we're proud of. Some will haunt us forever. The message here is, WE ARE WHAT WE CHOOSE TO BE.

Graham Brown.

In life, you have 3 CHOICES, Give UP. Give IN or Give IT your all. Anonymous

Happiness is a conscious choice, not an automatic response. Dailyquotes,com

Happiness is a choice; so choose to let go of things that frustrate you and start enjoying your life.

Picturequotes.com

HAPPINESS IS A CHOICE

CHOOSE IT EVERYDAY

YOUR ATTITUDE

+

YOUR CHOICE

=

YOUR LIFE

DAY 29
DO YOU WANT TO LIVE OR DIE?

Everybody dies, but not everybody lives. Anonymous

There was a hospital study done on 100 elderly people facing death close to their last breath.

They were asked to reflect on their life's biggest regret. Nearly all of them said thy regretted not the thing they did, but the things they didn't do. The risk they never took, the dreams they never pursue and how happy they would have been if they did.

IF I ASKED YOU WHAT WILL YOUR LAST WORD BE: Will it be, "If only I had…

This is a question I asked myself sometimes last year and that brought me close to writing this book. I didn't want my answer to be, "If only I had.

Writing this book is my dream come true, it is sharing my story with my world. Lessons learnt in life are not just for you but also for the universe.

If you choose to live, then live indeed.

Take every step to enjoy your life.

You owe yourself that much.

No one is going to do that for you.

You have to do that yourself.

Get up from bed everyday, sprang up with fresh energy to live.

Remember,

You are strong

You are powerful

You are indomitable…. Kenny Akindele-Akande

DAY 30

WHAT ARE YOUR OVERALL DECISIONS AFTER READING THIS BOOK WRITE THEM DOWN

DAY 31

START LIVING THAT HAPPY LIFE, STAY ON TOP OF THE GAME.

ACKNOWLEDGEMENT

I am dedicating this book to God Almighty for His amazing grace that He continuously bestowed on me, most especially in writing my first book.

I want to us dedicate it to my late parents, Rev S.A Akindele and Deaconess F.J Akindele {Nee Fayinto} for bringing me {and my siblings} up in the best way ever, the way of the Lord. To my sisters and my twin brother, I love you all.

And to my one and only PALS in the world, my humble and loving husband and kids. Thanks for giving me a conducive environment to fly.

I want to thank everyone that has been there for me in life, Daddy & Mummy Adegbolagun, who took care of my family and step-in as parent for when we lost our parents.

I want to also appreciate every dedicated member of Rev Akindele Endowment Funds, Liberty Evangelical Church {my childhood church} and the General Overseer, Pastor & Pastor Mrs Abegunde . The solid foundation in Christ you taught me has not left me till today, all glory to God.

To all my Spiritual and Professional Mentors, Mr Adams Adebola, Mr Agboola Cole and Dr Kolade Oni, you made an unforgettable impact in my life.

Relocating to the UK was a giant step in my life, but I never regretted it because of the lovely parent-in-laws I'm graced to have, Daddy & Mummy Akande and all my brothers and sisters-in-laws. Thanks for your love.

I will not forget my church, Fountain Of Peace Ministries and my Father-in-the Lord, Pastor {Dr} Mark Amadi for your love and support.

I acknowledge Dr. Mark Amadi, Dr. Ross Mckenzie and Simon Coulson for endorsing my book.

Thumbs up to all who supported me on this book journey, Book coach Tunji Ogunjimi {for teaching me book strategy and structure}, Ayo Akande {for connecting me with just the people I needed} and Abisoye Odutayo {for helping with proof-reading}. To Jide Popoola, Anthony Adu and Seun Ibironke for your advice and support.

My "Partner-In-Purpose and Happiness team" Blessing Theophilus-Israel, Titilayo Adeluola, Abimbola Anibaba, Tabitha Fanoiki, Bernadette Makinde, Abimbola Asagade, Bisi Yusuf, Tomiwa Atanda, Omowunmi Falade, Yinka Akinlagun and Kenny Agabaje for your prayers and support.

Shout out to all the ''SHE'' in my world, girls, ladies, and women, mothers, grand mothers.

To all my imminent readers, fans and sponsors especially to you reading this book right now, THANK YOU.

Printed in the United States
By Bookmasters